DAD - 2015
JOE

MW00605162

MAIL POUCH BARNS
OF WEST VIRGINIA

STEVE SHALUTA

Charleston, West Virginia

Quarrier Press
Charleston, WV

© 2010 Steve Shaluta

All rights reserved. No part of this book may be reproduced
in any form or in any means, electronic or mechanical,
including photocopying, recording, or by any information
storage and retrieval system, without permission
in writing from the publisher.

10 9 8 7 6 5 4 3 2 1

Printed in China

ISBN-13: 978-1-891852-67-1
ISBN-10: 1-891852-67-1

LCCN: 2009938202

Book and cover design by Mark S. Phillips

Distributed by:

West Virginia Book Company
1125 Central Avenue
Charleston, WV 25302
www.wvbookco.com

Dedication

For my lovely wife Vickie...
she understands my obsessions.

Introduction

As a professional outdoor photographer based in West Virginia, I frequently observed and enjoyed the many Mail Pouch barns around the state. I was struck by how many there were, and occasionally I would photograph an especially attractive or unusual one.

But that habit changed in 2003. I decided to locate and photograph all the existing Mail Pouch barns in West Virginia. I visited the headquarters of Mail Pouch Tobacco in Wheeling to obtain records of the locations of the painted Mail Pouch barns. Most of these barns were painted by the man known as "the last Mail Pouch barn painter," Harley Warrick. Records were limited, but the personnel at Mail Pouch Tobacco were extremely helpful, so with limited records in hand...off I went in search of my Mail Pouch treasures.

Most of the images in this book were photographed over a 2 ½ year period from 2003 to 2005. That's when I spent most weekends logging many miles in my search, traveling with my camera, notes and trusty atlas. During my search I realized that not only barns but many other types of buildings bore these wonderfully graphic and distinctive Mail Pouch advertisements. I decided to include in my quest any building or sign with a historical Mail Pouch advertisement painted on it. Anything painted by Harley was automatically included. After he retired from Mail Pouch, he continued to paint Mail Pouch barns and signs until his death in November 2000.

This book is not intended to be a historically precise record of every West Virginia Mail Pouch barn or sign ever painted. Instead, it represents my journey capturing these historic ads, my first one being in Webster County in 1986 (page 126). Although I have tried to find all the barns and signs in West Virginia, in all probability I have missed one or two. I have also included directions to each location, so this book can be used as a guide for the Mail Pouch enthusiast. Any barns or signs no longer standing will be noted in the caption although I'm sure more will have disappeared by the time you have read this.

To see additional images of West Virginia scenes and Mail Pouch barns or to purchase prints and books visit my website at ... **www.steveshaluta.com.**

Located along Rt. 250 in downtown Belington, Barbour County.

In Philippi, WV from the junction of Rt. 250 and Rt. 119, at the Philippi covered bridge, drive south on Rt. 250 for 2.2 miles. Turn right onto Old Rt. 250/23 and drive 2.4 miles. This barn was torn down in 2008.

Located in Philippi, Barbour County. From the junction of Rt. 250 and Rt. 119 at the Philippi covered bridge, drive south on Rt. 250 for 2.2 miles. Turn right onto Old Rt. 250/23 and drive 1.0 miles. Barn sits on east side of road.

Located in Belington, Barbour County. From the junction of Rt. 250 and Rt. 92 in Belington, drive north on Rt. 92 for 1.0 miles. Barn sits on west side of road.

Located in Philippi, Barbour County. From the junction of Rt. 250 and Rt. 119, at the Philippi covered bridge, drive south on Rt. 250 for 1.5 miles. Barn is on east side of the road down over a hill.

Located in Berkeley County. From the junction of Rt. 901 north and Rt. 9 in Hedgesville, drive west for 5.1 miles on Rt. 9. Barn sits on south side of the road.

Was located in Madison, Boone County, but torn down in 2007. From the Junction of Rt. 85 and Rt. 17 in Madison, drive south on Rt. 17 approximately 3 miles. Barn sat on east side of road.

Located at the Riverview Golf Course,
about 6 miles south of Madison on Rt. 17.
Boone County, WV.

Near Flatwoods, Braxton County. From the junction of I-79 Exit 67 (Flatwoods) and Rt. 19, drive north on Rt. 19 for 6.3 miles. Barn sits on the east side of the road up a small hollow.

Near Flatwoods, Braxton County. From the junction of I-79 Exit 67 (Flatwoods) and Rt. 19, drive north on Rt. 19 for 6.3 miles. Barn sits on the east side of the road up a small hollow.

Located in Huntington in Cabell County. At the corner of 6th Street and 8th Avenue, on the Goldsmit-Sydnor Wholesale building.

Located in the Central City section of Huntington in Cabell County. It is on the corner of West 14th and West 5th Streets.

Located along Rt. 60 in downtown Milton,
Cabell County, WV.

From I-64 at Milton, Cabell County, take Exit 28 (Milton CR 13) and drive to the junction of CR 13 and Rt. 60 at Milton. Drive east on Rt. 60 for 1.0 miles to Kilgore Creek Road, CR 16. Turn onto Kilgore Creek road under I-64 and drive .2 miles, where the barn sits in a field to the right.

From I-64 at Huntington, Cabell County, take Exit 11 (Hal Greer Blvd.). Turn south onto Rt. 10 and drive 2.8 miles. Barn is on the west side. (Mail Pouch sign can only be seen while driving north on Rt. 10). Very faded.

Located in Calhoun County. From the junction of Rt. 19-33 and Rt. 16 North, drive north on Rt. 16 for 9.6 miles. Barn sits on the west side of the road. (Note: See the word "WOW" ghosting through.)

Located in Calhoun County. From
the junction of Rt. 16 and Rt. 119 at
Arnoldsburg, drive north on Rt. 119 for
1.3 miles. Barn sits on east side of the
road. The sign is very hard to see, and the
ghosting "WOW" even more so.

Located in Calhoun County. From the junction of Rt. 19-33 and Rt. 16 North, drive north on Rt. 16 for 8.6 miles. Barn sits on the east side of the road.

Located in Calhoun County. From the junction of Rt. 16 and Rt. 33 in Arnoldsburg, west on Rt. 33 approximately 3.5 miles. Barn is located on the north side of the road. The Mail Pouch sign was located on west end of barn, but has been missing since February 2004.

Located in Calhoun County. From the junction of Rt. 16 and Rt. 33 in Arnoldsburg, drive west on Rt. 33 approximately 3.5 miles. Barn is located on the north side of the road. Mail Pouch sign is located on the east end of barn.

Located in Doddridge County. From Rt. 50 west of West Union, turn onto CR 50/30 (Sunnyside) and drive .7 miles. Barn sits on the west side of road.

Was located in Fayette County until 2009.
From junction of Rt. 19 and Rt. 60 (Ansted
exit), drive west on Rt. 60 for 2.2 miles.
Barn sat on south side of the road.

Was standing until 2009 in Fayette County. From junction of Rt. 19 and Rt. 60 (Ansted exit), west on Rt. 60 for 2.2 miles.

At Camp Washington Carver, near Babcock State Park in Fayette County. Two Mail Pouch signs are painted on this fence that surrounds a holding tank.

Located in Greenbrier County. From junction of I-64 Exit 156 (Sam Black Church) and Rt. 60, drive west on Rt. 60 for 2.5 miles to Crawley. Building sits on south side of the road. Mail Pouch sign can only be seen when driving east on Rt. 60.

Located in Greenbrier County. From I-64 Exit 161 (Alta), drive north on Rt. 12 for .2 miles to the junction of Rt. 12 and Rt. 60. Then drive on Rt. 60 for 3.8 miles. Barn sits on the north side of the road.

Located in Greenbrier County. From the junction of I-64 Exit 169 (Lewisburg) and Rt. 219, drive north on Rt. 219 for 4.8 miles. Barn sits on west side of the road.

Located in Hampshire County. From the junction of Rt. 29 north and Rt. 50, drive north on Rt. 29 for 7.1 miles (Slanesville). Barn sits on east side of the road.

Located in Hampshire County. From the junction of Rt. 50 and Rt. 220 South, drive east on Rt. 50 for 2.1 miles. Barn sits on north side of the road. (Mail Pouch signs on 2 ends and 1 side.)

Located in Hampshire County. From the junction of Rt. 50 and Rt. 29 North, drive east on Rt. 50 for 3.1 miles. Barn sits on the south side of the road. (Mail Pouch signs are on both ends of building.)

Located in Hampshire County. From the junction of Rt. 50 and Rt. 29 North, drive west on Rt. 50 for 3.7 miles. Barn sits on the north side of the road.

Located in Hampshire County. From the junction of Rt. 50 and Rt. 220 South, drive east on Rt. 50 for 3.0 miles. Barn sits on south side of the road. Barn is in very poor condition.

Located in Harrison County. From I-79 exit 105, drive toward Jane Lew to the junction of Rt. 19. Drive north on Rt. 19 approximately 4 miles. Barn sits on east side of the road. Original sign taken off old barn when demolished and placed on newly built barn.

Located in Harrison County. From I-79
Exit 105, drive toward Jane Lew to the
junction with Rt. 19. Drive north on Rt. 19
for 3.1 miles. Barn sits on east side of the
road. Mail Pouch signs on 2 ends.

Located in Jackson County. From the junction of Rt. 56 and Rt. 21, drive north on Rt. 21 for 2.4 miles. Barn sits on the west side of the road. Kentucky Club sign on the south end and Mail Pouch sign on the north end.

Located in Jackson County. From I-77 Exit 132 (Fairplain) drive south on Rt. 21 for 1.6 miles. Barn sits on west side of road.

Located in Jackson County. From the junction of Rt. 56 and Rt. 21, drive north on Rt. 21 for 4.8 miles. Barn sits on east side of road.

Located in Jackson County. From Exit 119 on I-77 (at Goldtown), drive north on Rt. 21 for .2 miles. Barn sits on west side of road.

Located in Jackson County. From the junction of Rt. 56 and Rt. 21, drive north on Rt. 21 for 10.1 miles. Barn sits on the west side of road.

Located in downtown Ravenswood,
Jackson County, at the corner of
Washington and Mulberry Streets.

Located in Jackson County. From I-77,
Exit 138 in Ripley, drive west on Rt. 33
for 5.1 miles. Turn left onto CR 5 (Evans
Road) and drive .8 miles. Barn sits on east
side of road. Mail Pouch sign can only be
seen when traveling north on CR 5.

Located in Jackson County.
From the junction of Rt. 56
and Rt. 21, drive north on Rt.
21 for 2.9 miles. Barn sits
on west side of road. Mail
Pouch sign appears on two
ends of the barn.

Located in Jackson County. From the junction of Rt. 56 and Rt. 21 at Sandyville, drive south on Rt. 21 for 4.1 miles. Barn sits on the east side of the road behind the West Virginia Forestry Association building. Barn is difficult to see from Rt. 21. Mail Pouch signs appear on two ends of the barn.

Located in Jackson County. From the junction of Rt. 56 and Rt. 21, drive north on Rt. 21 for 2.4 miles. Barn sits on the west side of the road. Kentucky Club sign appears on the south end and Mail Pouch sign on the north end.

Located in Jackson County. From I-77 at Exit 138 (Ripley), drive west on Rt. 33 for 3.5 miles. Barn sits on south side of road. Mail Pouch signs appear on two ends of the barn.

Located in Kanawha County. From I-79 at Exit 9, take CR 43 for 1.2 miles to the junction of CR 43 and Rt. 119. Drive north on Rt. 119 for 2.6 miles. Barn sits on the east side of the road.

Located in Kanawha County. From I-79 at
Exit 9 (Elkview), take CR 43 for 1.3 miles
to the junction of CR 43 and Rt. 119. Drive
north on Rt. 119 for 2.3 miles. Barn sits
on west side of road.

Located in Kanawha County. From the junction of I-79, Exit 1 (Mink Shoals), and Rt. 119, drive north on Rt. 119 for 2.0 miles to Crede Drive. Garage is located behind a house at 3610 Crede Drive.

Close-up of Harley Warrick's initials that appear on this Mail Pouch sign. The owner related the story that Harley was at an art and craft show in Charleston, when the owner asked how much he would charge to paint his garage. Obviously a price was agreed upon.

Located in the museum at the West Virginia Cultural Center, Capitol Complex in Charleston.

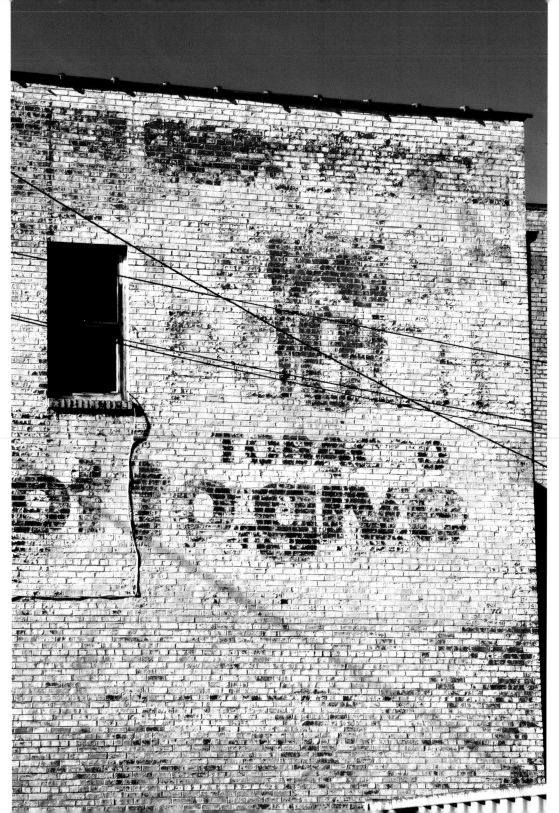

Located in downtown St. Albans, Kanawha County. This sign could be seen until it was painted over in 2008. It was near the corner of Main and 3rd Streets, on the side of St. Albans' Florist building.

Located in Lewis County. From the junction of Rt. 19 and Routes 33/119 in Weston, drive south on Rt. 119 for 7.1 miles. Barn sits in field on east side of road.

Located in Lincoln County. From the junction of Rt. 3 and Rt. 34, near Hamlin. Drive north on Rt. 34 for .8 miles. The barn sits on the west side of the road. Sign can only be seen while driving south on Rt. 34.

Located in Yawkey in Lincoln County.
From the junction of Rt. 214 and Rt. 3,
drive west on Rt. 3 for .9 miles. Barn sits
on north side of road.

Located in Lincoln County. From the junction of Rt. 3 and Rt. 10 in West Hamlin, drive 1.1 miles south on Rt. 10. The barn is located on the west side of Rt. 10. Mail Pouch sign appears on two ends. Note "WOW" sign ghosting through.

Located in Marion County. From the junction of Rt. 250 and Rt. 19 in downtown Fairmont, drive north on Rt. 19 approximately 1-2 miles. Building sits on west side. Sign can only be seen when driving south on Rt. 19.

*Located along Rt. 19 in downtown
Monongah in Marion County. Barn is on
east side of the road.*

This Mail Pouch sign appears on the side of a building on the corner of Main and North Streets in the town of Cameron, in Marshall County.

On a rather forlorn spot in Benwood, in
Marshall County, at the corner of 8th and
McMechen Streets.

Another Mail Pouch in McMechen, Marshall County, is on 6th Street near the Marshall Street corner.

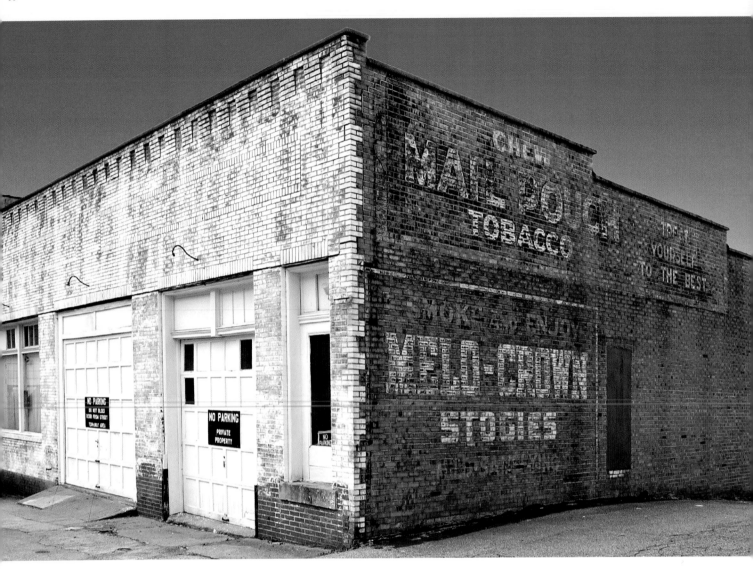

Competing with an ad for Melo-Crown Stogies, this Mail Pouch ad is on the corner of 10th and Marshall Streets, in McMechen, Marshall County.

In Marshall County, from the junction of Routes 88 North and 88 South in Bethlehem, drive south on Rt. 88 for 1.1 miles to Frazier Avenue (CR 3). Turn on Frazier Avenue and drive .1 miles. Barn sits on west side of the road.

*From the junction of Rt. 88 and Rt. 250,
drive south on Rt. 250 for 5.1 miles. Barn
sits on the east side of the road and is
very hard to see the one Mail Pouch sign
on the side.*

Located in Marshall County. From the junction of Rt. 250 and Rt. 891 north of Cameron, drive north on Rt. 250 for .4 miles. Barn sits on the west side of the road. Mail Pouch sign can only be seen when driving south on Rt. 250.

*Located in Marshall County on Rt. 250
at the junction with Rt. 891, north of
Cameron. Barn sits on the east side of the
road. The roof collapsed in January 2004.*

Located in Marshall County. From the junction of Rt. 88 and Rt. 250, drive south on Rt. 250 for 4.3 miles. Barn sits on the east side of the road at Pleasant Valley. Sign can only be seen when driving south on Rt. 250.

Located in Marshall County. From the junction of Rt. 891 and Rt. 250, drive south on Rt. 250 for .5 miles. Barn sits on east side of the road down over hill.

From the junction of Rt. 2 and Rt. 35 at
Point Pleasant in Mason County, drive
south on Rt. 2 for 9.2 miles. Barn sits on
west side of the road.

In Mason County, from the junction of Routes 2 and 62 drive north on Rt. 2 for approximately 6 miles. Barn is located on the east side of the road. Two sides are Mail Pouch; one is Kentucky Club.

In Mason County, from the junction of Routes 2 and 35 in Point Pleasant, drive east on Rt. 35 for approximately 17 miles. Barn sits on the north side of the road. Mail Pouch signs appear on 2 ends of the barn.

Located along Rt. 2 in Glenwood, Mason County, on the east side of the road along the railroad tracks. Sign is extremely faded.

In Mason County, from the junction of Routes 2 and 62 South near Point Pleasant, drive south on Rt. 62 for 6.3 miles. Barn sits on east side of road.

Collapsed and removed in 2008. In
Monongalia County, from the junction of
Rt. 19 and Rt. 7, drive west on Rt. 7 for
7.8 miles. Barn sat on the north side of
the road. It had Mail Pouch signs on two
ends.

Monongalia County. From the junction of Routes 218 North and 7 in Blacksville, drive west on Rt. 7 for 4.2 miles. Barn sits on south side of road. Mail Pouch signs are on two ends.

Located in Maidsville, Monongalia County. From the junction of Rt. 19 and Rt. 100 in Westover, drive north toward Maidsville on Rt. 100 for 4.9 miles. Barn sits on the east side of the road.

Located In Monroe County. From the junction of Routes 219 and 60 in downtown Lewisburg, drive south on Rt. 219 for 15.7 miles to the junction with Rt. 3 at Pickaway. Drive west on Rt. 3 for .1 miles. Barn sits on the north side of road. Mail Pouch sign very faded.

From the junction of Routes 41 and 39
in downtown Summersville in Nicholas
County, drive west on Rt. 39 for 6.8 miles.
Barn sits on south side of the road.

From the junction of Routes 41 and 39 in downtown Summersville in Nicholas County, drive west on Rt. 39 for 7.8 miles. Barn sits on north side of the road.

From the junction of Routes 19 and 41
South at the Mt. Nebo exit in Nicholas
County, drive south on Rt. 41 for .5 miles.
Barn sits on east side of road.

From the junction of Routes 19 and 55 East at the Muddlety exit in Nicholas County, drive east on Rt. 55 for 1.1 miles. Barn sits on south side of road. Mail Pouch sign—very faded—can only be seen when driving west on Rt. 55.

The Mail Pouch headquarters and factory in Wheeling. Sign appears on the corner of 40th and Jacob Streets, and identifies Bloch Brothers Tobacco, owners.

The Mail Pouch headquarters and factory in Wheeling. Sign appears on two sides of building at the corner of 40th and Water Streets.

*In Ohio County, at the junction of I-70,
Exit 5 (to Elm Grove/Tridelphia), and Rt.
40, drive east on Rt. 40 for 6.5 miles.
Garage sits on the south side of the road.
Mail Pouch signs appear on two ends.*

Located in Wheeling on Jacob Street between 35th and 36th streets.

This 1993 photo shows a Mail Pouch barn in Pocahontas County on the west side of the road along Rt. 219 near Slatyfork. The barn was torn down in the mid-to-late 1990s.

This Mail Pouch barn was located in
Pocahontas County on the east side of
the road along Rt. 219 near the junction
of Rt. 66 and Rt. 219 near Snowshoe. The
barn collapsed and was subsequently
removed in the mid 1990s.

In Preston County, from I-68 Exit 23 and the junction of Rt. 26, drive south on Rt. 26 for 2.3 miles. Barn sits on east side of road, and can only be seen when driving north on Rt. 26.

From the junction of Rt. 219 and Rt. 50 in Red House, Maryland, drive west on Rt. 50 for 4.6 miles. Barn sits on north side of the road just east of Cathedral State Park in Preston County. Mail Pouch signs appear twice on the front and once on the east end of the barn.

In Preston County, from the junction of Rt. 50 and Rt. 92 near Fellowsville, drive 9.4 miles on Rt. 92 north. Barn sits on east side of the road, with Mail Pouch signs at each end.

Located in Preston County. From the junction of Rt. 219 and Rt. 50 in Red House, MD, drive west on Rt. 50 for 5.5 miles. Barn sits on the south side of the road, east of Aurora. Mail Pouch sign can only be seen while driving east on Rt. 50.

In Putnam County, from the junction of
Rt. 62 and Eleanor Circle 35/13 in Eleanor
(the road to county park), drive .3 miles
on 35/13 and turn right onto Park Road.
Drive 1.0 miles to the barn, located at the
Putnam County Fairgrounds.

Near Hurricane in Putnam County, from the junction of Rt. 34 and Rt. 60, drive 2 miles east on Rt. 60. Barn is located on north side of road.

Near Hurricane in Putnam County, from
the junction of Rt. 34 and Rt. 60, drive .2
miles west on Rt. 60. Barn is located on
north side of the road.

In Randolph County, from Rt. 219 (Corridor H) north of Elkins, take Kerns Rd.-Parsons exit. Drive north on Rt. 219 for 1.3 miles. Barn sits on west side of the road. Mail Pouch signs appear on one end and one side.

Located in Randolph County. From the junction of Rt. 219 and Rt. 250 at Huttonsville, drive south on Rt. 219 for 13.1 miles to the junction of Rt. 219 and Rt. 15. Barn sits on west side of the road.

In Randolph County, from the junction of Rt. 219 and Rt. 250 at Huttonsville, drive south on Rt. 219 for 3.5 miles. Barn sits on west side of the road.

In Randolph County, from the junction of Rt. 219 and Rt. 250 at Huttonsville, drive south on Rt. 219 for 6.2 miles. Barn sits on east side of road. Mail Pouch signs appear on one end and one side.

In Randolph County, from the junction of Rt. 219 and Rt. 250 at Huttonsville, drive south on Rt. 219 for 8.8 miles. Barn sits on west side of the road.

In Randolph County, from the junction of Rt. 219 and Rt. 250 at Huttonsville, drive south on Rt. 219 for 9.8 miles. Barn sits on east side of the road. Mail Pouch signs appear on two ends and one side.

In Ritchie County, from the junction of Rt. 50 and Rt. 16 at Ellenboro, drive south on Rt. 16 for 5.4 miles (south of Harrisville). Barn sits on west side of road. Note "WOW" ghosting through sign. Mail Pouch signs appear on each end.

Located in Ritchie County. From the junction of I-77 Exit 176 and Rt. 50, drive east on Rt. 50 for 15.5 miles to CR 50/2 on left (no road sign). Mail Pouch sign can only be seen while going west. Note "WOW" sign ghosting though.

In Ritchie County, from junction of Rt. 50 and CR 50/34 (Nutter Farm Rd.), drive east on CR 50/34 for 4.5 miles. Barn sits on south side of road.

In Ritchie County, from the junction of Rt. 74 South and Rt. 74 North in Pennsboro, drive north on Rt. 74 for 5.0 miles. Barn sits on east side of road.

In Ritchie County, from the junction of Rt. 50 and CR 10 (Toll Gate exit), drive .3 miles to a stop sign. Turn left and drive .4 miles to another stop sign. Make sharp right and drive .3 miles to a dead end. Barn sits on the left side of the road.

*In Roane County, from the junction of
Rt. 33 and Rt. 14 in Spencer, drive north
on Rt. 14 for 3.7 miles. Barn sits on west
side of road behind white house and a red
barn. (Difficult to see from road).*

In Roane County, from the junction of Rt. 33 and Rt. 14 in Spencer, drive north on Rt. 14 for 6.0 miles. Barn sits in field on west side of the road.

In Roane County, from the junction of
Rt. 14 and Rt. 33 in Spencer, drive east
on Rt. 33 for 6.0 miles. Barn sits on north
side of road. Sign can only be seen while
driving west on Rt. 33. Another Mail
Pouch sign is on small garage north and
east of the barn.

In Roane County, from the junction of Rt. 33 and Rt. 119 in Spencer, drive south on Rt. 119 for 5.5 miles. The barn was on the left side of the road, but was torn down in 2006.

In Roane County, from the junction of Rt.
33 and Rt. 119 in Spencer, drive south on
Rt. 119 for 3.7 miles. Barn is located on
east side of road. Mail Pouch signs are on
two ends and one side.

In Taylor County in downtown Flemington, 100 yards east of the junction of Rt. 76 and CR 13 on CR 13. On the south side of the road, the Mail Pouch sign can only be seen when driving west on CR 13.

In Taylor County on East Main Street in Grafton, this Mail Pouch sign was uncovered only when the adjacent building was torn down.

In Taylor County on Latrobe Street in Grafton.

Located in Taylor County. Latrobe Street in Grafton. Sign is very faded. Directly across the lot is another building with a faded Mail Pouch sign.

Located in Taylor County. Latrobe Street in Grafton. Sign is very faded.

In Taylor County, from the junction of Rt. 50 and Rt. 119, drive north on Rt. 119 for 2.0 miles. Barn sits on west side of the road across from the Grafton Drive-in Theater.

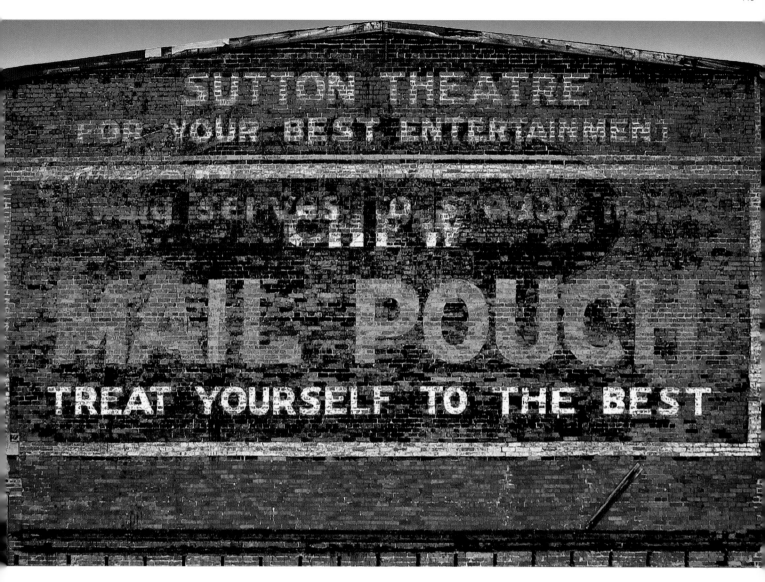

Located in Tucker County in small town of Thomas.

In Tyler County along Rt. 2 in town of Friendly. Barn sits on the east side of the road. Mail Pouch sign can only be seen when driving north on Rt. 2. Sign was repainted in 2006.

In Upshur County, from the junction of Rt. 33 and Rt. 119 at Buckhannon, drive north on Rt. 119 for 4.0 miles. Barn sat on the west side of the road until 2009.

This sign can be found on the Farnsworth Building on Main Street in downtown Buckhannon, Upshur County, across the street from the Courthouse.

In Upshur County, from the junction of Rt. 119 and Rt. 33 at Buckhannon, drive east on Rt. 33 for 3.5 miles to old Rt. 33 (Rt. 151). At Rt. 151 turn right. Drive east on Rt. 151 for 3.0 miles. Barn sits on south side of the road.

In Wayne County, from the junction of
Rt. 152 and Rt. 37 at Echo, drive 1.7
miles west on Rt. 37. Barn is located on
the south side of the road on a hillside
hidden by trees. Mail Pouch sign appears
on one end and one side; Kentucky Club
sign also appears on one end.

In Wayne County, from the junction of Rt. 152 and Rt. 75, drive west on Rt. 75 for 4.2 miles. Barn sits on the north side of the road. Faint Mail Pouch signs can be seen on the front and on one side.

In Wayne County from the junction of Rt.
52 and Rt. 75, drive east on Rt. 75 for 2.2
miles. Barn sits on the south side of the
road. Mail Pouch sign appears on one
end and one side.

In Wayne County, from the junction of Rt. 52 and Rt. 75, drive east on Rt. 75 for 1.1 miles. Barn sits on the north side of the road. A shed roof overhangs the Mail Pouch sign, which can only be seen when driving west on Rt. 75.

In Wayne County, from the junction of Rt. 152 and Rt. 37 at Echo, drive south on Rt. 152 for 17.2 miles. Barn sits on east side of the road and can only be seen if traveling north on Rt. 152.

When entering Wayne County from the north, at the junction of Rt. 152 and Rt. 37 at Echo, drive south on Rt. 152 for 16.2 miles to Dunlow. Barn sits on the east side.

This photo was taken in 1986—I call it the OUCH barn, which is no longer standing. It was located along Rt. 20 in Hacker Valley in Webster County.

In Wetzel County, from the junction of
Rt. 250 and Rt. 7 in Hundred, drive 7 - 8
miles north on Rt. 250. Barn sits on the
east side of the road.

*In Wirt County, from the junction of Rt.
33 and Rt. 14 in Spencer, drive north on
Rt. 14 for 14.6 miles. Barn sits on the east
side of the road.*

In Wirt County, from the junction of Rt. 33 and Rt. 14 in Spencer, drive north on Rt. 14 for 14.6 miles to Lee Run Road, 14/18. Turn right onto Lee Run Road and drive .1 miles. Barn sits on right side of the road.

In Wirt County, from the junction of Rt. 5 and Rt. 14 in Elizabeth, drive south on Rt. 14 for 8.6 miles. Barn sits on west side of road.

In Wirt County, from the junction of I-77, Exit 147 and Rt. 47, drive east on Rt. 47 for 13.4 miles. Barn sits on north side of road.

Located In Wood County in Parkersburg, this Mail Pouch sign is located near the railroad tracks on Green Street and the corner of 7th Street at rear of building.

In Wood County, from the junction of I-79 at Exit 179 and Rt. 68, drive south on Rt. 68 for 2.8 miles to CR 14/16 (Rosemar Road). Turn right onto Rosemar Rd. and drive 2.8 miles to Ridge Road CR 4. Turn right onto Ridge Road and drive .6 miles. Barn sits on the left side of the road. The Six family dismantled this barn in Ohio and rebuilt it on this location.

In Wood County, from I-77, Exit 161 at Rockport, drive north on Rt. 21 for 1.7 miles. Barn sits on east side of the road.

This barn is located in Wood County. From the junction of Rt. 14 and Rt. 21 at Mineral Wells, drive south on Rt. 21 for 1.6 miles. Barn sits on east side of road.

In Wood County, from the junction of Rt.
50 and I-77, Exit 176, drive east on Rt. 50
for 1 mile to Rt. 50/38 (Red Hill Road).
Drive east on Rt. 50/38 for 1.8 miles. Barn
sits on south side of the road. Mail Pouch
signs appear on two ends.

Located on Avery Street in Parkersburg, Wood County, between 3rd and 4th Streets. Two Mail Pouch signs on one building, the sign above being on the southwest end, and (above left) the southeast end.

Located in Wood County. From the junction of Rt. 68 south of Parkersburg and Lake Washington Road (CR 34), drive 1.3 miles on CR 34. Turn onto Smitherman Road (CR 36/1), and drive .2 miles. Barn is on the left.

Located in Wood County. From the junction of Rt. 892 and Jewell Road (CR 30/1), south of Parkersburg, drive .3 miles out Jewell Road. Barn sits on right side of the road.

Vickie Shaluta Photo

Steve Shaluta is a former railroad engineer who grew up in Grafton. In 1985 he decided to turn his hobby of photography into a full time career, leaving behind 14 1/2 years as a railroad engineer. Steve has had literally thousands of images published and his framed art prints can be found in businesses and homes throughout the Appalachian and Mid-Atlantic regions. With over 350 magazine covers, 8 books and numerous images published in calendars and books, his decision to change careers was a good one. His most recent project, **West Virginia Beauty: Familiar & Rare**, is a coffee table book collaboration with writer Jeanne Mozier.

www.steveshaluta.com